A Smart Kid's Guide to
Doing Internet Research

David J. Jakubiak

PowerKiDS press™

New York

Published in 2010 by The Rosen Publishing Group, Inc.
29 East 21st Street, New York, NY 10010

First Edition

Editor: Amelie von Zumbusch
Book Design: Julio Gil
Photo Researcher: Jessica Gerweck

Photo Credits: Cover Shutterstock.com; p. 5 Gazimal/Getty Images; p. 6 Patryce Bak/Getty Images; p. 9 © www.iStockphoto.com/Lisa F. Young; p. 10 Alex Mares-Manton/Getty Images; p. 13 © Jim Cummins/Corbis; p. 14 © Gerald French/Corbis; p. 17 Bruce Laurance/Getty Images; p. 18 Jim Esposito/Getty Images; p. 21 © www.iStockphoto.com/Sean Locke.

Library of Congress Cataloging-in-Publication Data

Jakubiak, David J.
    A smart kid's guide to doing Internet research / David J. Jakubiak. — 1st ed.
        p. cm. — (Kids online)
    Includes index.
    ISBN 978-1-4042-8116-5 (lib. bdg.) — ISBN 978-1-4358-3352-4 (pbk.) —
ISBN 978-1-4358-3353-1 (6-pack)
    1. Internet research—Juvenile literature. I. Title.
    ZA4228.J35 2010
    001.4'202854678—dc22
                                                2009002879

Manufactured in the United States of America

CPSIA Compliance Information: Batch #WR904211PK: For Further Information contact Rosen Publishing, New York, New York at 1-800-237-9932

Contents

Research Everything

Do you ever use the Internet to find pictures of puppies? Have you ever looked up the words to a song online? If you have, then you have done Internet research!

Searching for songs or pictures on the Internet is a form of Internet research. Looking up facts online for school reports is Internet research, too. The Internet is a great tool for getting information, or facts. To find something online, though, you have to know what you are looking for. You also have to know how to find it. Knowing how to do online research can help you learn about anything that interests you, from hockey and hopscotch to hippos and hedgehogs.

The Internet makes doing research easy. You can learn about many subjects, such as music, sports, history, science, cars, movies, math, pets, and wild animals, online.

The World Wide Web lets you learn about the world from your own living room. The Web has sites that are based in hundreds of different countries.

The World Wide Web

The World Wide Web is made up of all the Web sites on the Internet. This makes it a powerful tool. Web sites can offer both the history of a **topic** and the latest news. For example, you can read about recent happenings at the White House and learn about all the past presidents of the United States at www.whitehouse.gov/kids.

While many sites on the Internet can be used for research, not everything you read online is true. Some sites list people's opinions instead of facts. Other sites belong to companies that are more interested in selling you something than in giving you good information. Figure out if a Web site is a good **source** before you believe anything the site says.

An Engine for Your Search

If you do not know where to start your Internet research, try a search engine. A search engine checks **millions** of Web sites for words you ask it to find. Then it lists Web sites that use those words. There are many search engines. Some common search engines are Google, Yahoo! Search, and Ask Kids. Sometimes using different search engines will give you different results.

With the help of a trusted adult, find some search engines. Ask the adult to use search-engine tools to block sites that are not safe for kids. Then, try some searches to see which search engines work best.

The computers in most libraries or schools are set up to block sites that are not meant for kids. This makes libraries and schools good places to do Internet research.

9

Putting in several keywords will often give you more exact results. If you need help coming up with keywords for your search, you can always ask a friend for ideas.

Get That Engine Running!

Search engines find only what you ask them to find. This makes picking the best words to search for very important. When picking **keywords**, think about exactly what you want to know.

If you want to learn about how tadpoles become frogs, a search for "tadpoles" will get more than a million results. Every site with the word "tadpoles" will show up, even clothing stores and rock bands named Tadpoles. Finding what you really want can be hard when there are so many sites. Instead, try a search for the keywords "tadpoles become frogs." This will leave out most of the extra sites and let you get to work.

Other Starting Points

There may be times when your first stop in doing Internet research will be your online classroom. Does your class have a Web site? If it does, use it. Ask your teacher what kinds of things you can find on the site. You may be able to use it to find reading lists or homework. Your teacher may set up **links** for you to use, too.

Try to find out if your school or library has a **subscription** to an online **encyclopedia**, such as www.worldbookonline.com or www.britannica.com. These sites have articles written by **experts**. Online encyclopedias let you search many topics, such as science, art, and social studies.

Many teachers are happy to sit down with their students and show them how to find Web sites that have information that is useful for school reports.

13

The San Diego Zoo is home to many interesting animals, such as these elephants. The zoo also has a great Web site. The site's address is www.sandiegozoo.org.

Go to the Source

When you are trying to find information online, think about people or groups that might know about what you are researching. A **museum** or zoo site can be a great source of information. If you are looking for information about a country, see if it has an **embassy** with a Web site.

Some sites, like that of the Field Museum, in Chicago, have experts to whom you can e-mail questions. Always check with your teacher, mother, father, or guardian before e-mailing someone you do not know. If you get an e-mail back from an expert, remember to say thank you.

Whom to Trust

Not every site is good for research. Some sites offer mostly opinion. Other sites were meant to make people laugh, not to supply information. Certain sites even have untrue information.

A site's address offers clues to its research value. You can generally trust government sites, which end in ".gov" and school sites, which end in ".edu." Sites ending in ".org" can be good or bad. For example, the site of the American Museum of Natural History, www.amnh.org, is a great source. On the other hand, the site www.wikipedia.org should not be used for schoolwork. This site has up-to-date information, but anybody can add to it. Therefore, it sometimes has mistakes or jokes.

You should always think carefully
about how trustworthy a site is before you gather
information from it to use in a report.

Do not believe everything that you see online.
Sites that sell things sometimes make crazy and untrue claims
about the things that their products can do.

Learning or Buying?

Sites that sell things are not generally good sources of information. These sites are online to make money, not to supply information. Sites ending in ".com" are often run by companies or people who want you to buy something.

Some people pay to have their sites shown when search engines do certain searches. For example, the site of a company that sells computers may appear on the **screen** when someone searches for "computers." Links to these sites are easy to spot. They are often found in a shaded box or placed to the side of the links found by the search engine.

Keeping Track

The more research you do online, the more information you will find. You can keep track of everything by printing the Web pages you use. When you are writing a report, always list the addresses of the Web pages from which you got your information. Never copy things from a Web site word for word. If you copy words from a site exactly, you are using someone else's work. Instead, write your report in your own words.

The Internet is a great source of information. Knowing how to do Internet research will help you in school and in life. If you are ready to learn, get ready to search!

class 204
September 22

A+

Report on
Mark Twain's
*The Adventures of
Tom Sawyer*

If you are writing a book report, you
can use the Internet to find out more about the book's au
the time at which the book was written.

Safety Tips

- Ask your mother, father, guardian, or teacher before visiting a site for research.

- Keep a list of good sites to use for research.

- **Bookmark** the search engine you like best and the sites that you use most often.

- If you want to find words in an exact order, place keywords in quotation marks when you are doing a search.

- If you are unsure if you can trust the information on a site, ask your teacher before you use facts from the site in a report.

- Never enter your e-mail address, name, age, or other information on a site before asking a trusted adult.

- Librarians can help you do research both online and using books.

Glossary

bookmark (BUHK-mahrk) To save the addresses of Web sites in a browser.

embassy (EM-buh-see) An official home and office of a certain country in another country.

encyclopedia (in-sy-kluh-PEE-dee-uh) Something with information about many subjects.

experts (EK-sperts) People who know a lot about a subject.

keywords (KEE-wurdz) Words that are used in a search.

links (LINKS) Addresses that take you to Web sites when you click on them.

millions (MIL-yunz) Thousand of thousands.

museum (myoo-ZEE-um) A place where art or historical pieces are safely kept for people to see and to study.

screen (SKREEN) The flat part of a computer that shows words and pictures.

source (SORS) Something that gives facts or knowledge.

subscription (sub-SKRIP-shun) An agreement to receive and to pay for something.

topic (TAH-pik) The subject of a piece of writing.

Index

Web Sites

Due to the changing nature of Internet links, PowerKids Press has developed an online list of Web sites related to the subject of this book. This site is updated regularly. Please use this link to access the list: www.powerkidslinks.com/onlin/research/